Climbing
Anchors
Field Guide

HOW TO CLIMB™ SERIES

Climbing Anchors
Field Guide

JOHN LONG and BOB GAINES

FALCONGUIDES ®

GUILFORD, CONNECTICUT
HELENA, MONTANA

AN IMPRINT OF THE GLOBE PEQUOT PRESS

FALCONGUIDES

Photos © Bob Gaines unless otherwise noted
Illustrations © Mike Clelland

Library of Congress Cataloging-in-Publication Data is available.
ISBN 978-0-7627-4504-3

Manufactured in the United States of America
First Edition/First Printing

Contents

Introduction

Climbing Anchors Field Guide is a companion guide to *Climbing Anchors*. Many readers reported the following experience: They would study anchor fundamentals in the large book (or prior anchor manuals), but when they ventured onto the rock and had to work strictly from memory, they sometimes struggled to remember the details. They also found that toting *Climbing Anchors* to the cliffside was neither practical nor desired. Tote this book instead. That's what it was made for.

Efficient use of this manual hinges on a complete understanding of the principles behind solid anchor construction, concepts that *Climbing Anchors* covers in great detail. Without understanding the why of it all, the most you can do is try to replicate what is shown in the photos. Understanding the critical theories behind anchoring allows you to improvise on a general theme—an essential skill since the setups in the photos are largely site specific and won't exactly translate to other cracks and faces. Every belay requires a leader to change up the details as the rock dictates, a potentially sketchy venture if you don't understand how it all works. So bone up on the theory in *Climbing Anchors*, and bust this out at the crags as a visual reference and reminder.

Aside from the photos, accompanying information is often presented via bullet points as a means of recollecting some of the key concepts detailed in *Climbing Anchors*. The bullet points are applied, practical information, but they are not a substitute for thoroughly studying the theories and principles of anchor dynamics as explained in the full text. In other words, *Climbing Anchors Field Guide* is not intended as a stand-alone instructional book. Those who use it as such do so at their own peril.

John Long and Bob Gaines

BASIC ANCHOR BUILDING FACTS:

- "Perfect" rarely exists in real world climbing anchors.

- No single rigging technique will work in every situation.

- Trad climbers must efficiently improvise on a handful of anchor building techniques.

- The ability to improvise requires a thorough understanding of basic principles.

- Climbing anchors always involve compromises—the trick is to understand what you should and should not compromise at a given place on the rock.

SIMPLE ANCHORS

CHAPTER ONE
Natural Anchors

NATURAL ANCHORS ARE:

1. Anything the environment provides—trees, blocks, horns of rock, etc.

2. Often more secure than gear-built anchors.

3. Typically easy and fast to arrange.

4. Multidirectional (can be loaded from any direction).

5. By and large environmentally friendly.

WHEN ANCHORING TO A TREE . . .

☐ Make sure it is alive.

☐ Use slings or a cordelette instead of rope to tie it off.

☐ Tie it off as low as possible to reduce leverage.

Anchoring to a Tree

Incorrect. When pulled straight out on, this setup will stress the relatively weak gate of the carabiner.

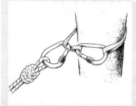

Slightly better, but the sling is overly stressed.

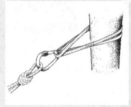

Okay. The sling configuration is strong, but the sling is loose and can easily slip around on the tree. Slide it down around the base for more security.

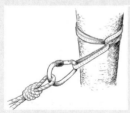

Okay. The girth-hitch keeps the runner from slipping on the tree.

By tying this cordelette off with a figure eight, it essentially becomes redundant, with two loops around the tree. The doubled, power point clip-in helps prevent improper loading of the biner. In all such setups, try to keep the inside angle of the cord/sling less than 90 degrees to avoid load multiplication.

The downside of keeping the inside angle less than 90 degrees is that the longer slings add slack to the system, and unless the tie-in remains under tension (by the belayer leaning off the anchor), the sling(s) can migrate down the tree trunk—not necessarily a bad thing with this atomic bombproof anchor. However, as a general practice, after you arrange protection/anchors, you don't want them to move—at all—till removal.

REMEMBER . . .

- Only their mass and position keep boulders and blocks in place.

- To serve as secure anchors, boulders and blocks must be sufficiently large and totally immovable.

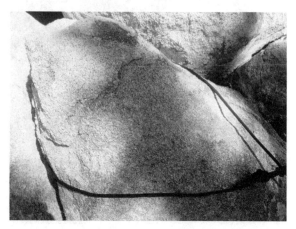

This block is well situated, and is bomber for the direction of pull for which it is rigged. As always, appraising the integrity of a natural rock anchor involves judgment. Carefully examine for cracks in the block. And most importantly, how well is the block attached to the main rock structure? If you decide to use a detached block, how big is it: the size of your car or the size of your boom box? Does it rest on a flat platform or a sloping shelf? As a general rule, many climbers avoid rigging anchors off detached blocks and flakes.

This detached block is gigantic, roughly the size of an out-house, but is precariously perched on a pedestal slim and angled. The crack between the block and the main wall will readily accept camming devices, but remember this: When you hear about catastrophic anchor failure, the number one cause is bad rock, where someone has committed to a single crack system in dubious rock, or perhaps a tragically loose flake or a detached block. Even the best placements are no better than the rock they are set in.

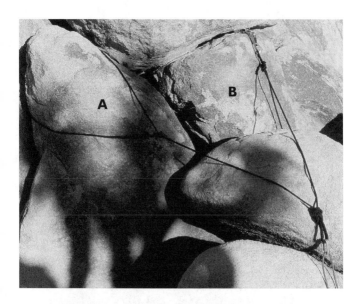

This TR rig consists of A) a natural rock bollard, and B) two camming devices in a horizontal crack. The anchor system is pre-equalized, featuring a static extension rope tied with a double-loop figure eight at the power point. The rope is attached with two oval carabiners, gates opposed and reversed.

Arranging a clean and simple anchor is sometimes tricky among such jumbled terrain. Here the climber decided where she wanted the power point and worked backward from there. The whole rig hangs nicely over the edge, and the use of the static rope is good for added abrasion resistance. The rock structure at A is beefy and well attached to the main rock structure. The two cams at B are solid placements, but if you scrutinize the structure, they are actually underneath a massive, detached block. The use of two oval carabiners opposed and reversed is adequate, but many climbing schools and outdoor programs use three oval carabiners, gates opposed and reversed, as their standard operating procedure.

WHATEVER THE ROCK FEATURE . . .

Look out for sharp edges.

Test the security of the feature by thumping it with the heel of your hand. Anything that wiggles or sounds hollow is suspect.

Look for surrounding cracks.

Tie off as close to the main wall as possible, to reduce leverage.

Tie off with runners, slip-knotting if the form is rounded.

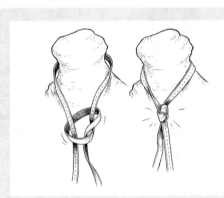

Using a slip-knot to sling a horn.

The climbers who made the decision to rap from this flake were lucky they lived to drive home. The structure is completely detached and precariously perched. Structural integrity is paramount when using natural rock anchors, and this one lacks it altogether. This is like building your house on quicksand. Remember: Slings around an "anchor" do not vouchsafe their security.

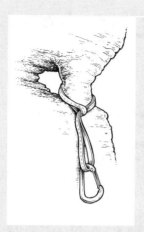

A tunnel girth-hitched with a runner.

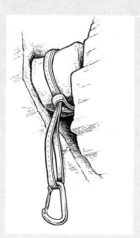

A girth-hitched chockstone. Make sure the hitch is tight around the chockstone and pulled snug against itself so it won't slip if stressed.

CHAPTER TWO

Passive Chocks

■ TAPERS

BASIC RULES OF PLACING A GOOD TAPER

- The taper has to be bigger—if only a bit—than the section of crack below where it is lodged.

- Slot the taper that most closely corresponds to the geometry of the crack.

- Whenever possible, set the taper where the crack not only pinches off in the downward direction but also in the outward direction.

- Orient the taper so the cable or sling points in the expected direction of pull/loading.

- Try to get the majority of the nut set against the rock, maximizing the amount of surface contact.

- Avoid endwise placements if possible, as they tend to be less secure.

- If you have a choice, go with the bigger taper, as it is generally more secure, with more surface area contacting the rock.

- Make sure the placement is well seated, with no movement or rattle when weighted by hand.

Both sides of this Stopper have great surface contact, and the constriction of the crack corresponds with the shape of the taper.

Like a man in the wrong-sized trousers, this Black Diamond Stopper does not fit the slot. A desirable placement would involve a larger Stopper normally placed (rather than end-wise), with the main faces of the chock flush with the walls of the crack. This nut has all the earmarks of sketchy pro: poor surface contact, susceptibility to an outward force plucking it from the crack and instability from sitting on the flat base of the nut. On a scale of 1 to 10 (10 being bomber), this Stopper is about a 2.

This Metolius Curve Nut has great flushness on the right wall of the crack, but the left side has negligible surface contact on gritty, grainy rock. Dicey! Because endwise placements are generally less stable, always strive to get a flush fit with as much surface contact as possible.

According to Metolius, the design of Curve Nuts, while not technically "offset," gives them added stability in flares. If you should wiggle this nut around a bit, you'd likely find an ideal placement—that's how it usually works. Few cracks are perfectly parallel sided, and slight repositioning can change a marginal placement to something much better—or worse.

This Stopper is flush on the left side, but the right side has only about 50 percent surface contact, plus the crack opens up immediately below the placement. This placement is *not* bomber—maybe good enough to hang off, but if this Stopper was all that was keeping you from hitting the deck, you'd best quickly look for other placements.

This Stopper is wedged in a bottleneck. In a straight, downward pull, it simply cannot be pulled through the constriction. But the left side of the chock protrudes slightly from the crack, and the right side is less than 50 percent flush. These types of placements are easily dislodged from the crack with even nominal outward force, as the surface contact is minimal and the crack opens up above the placement. When making such placements, a slight downward jerk will get the nut set well enough to withstand upward and outward forces while not making the placement difficult to clean. If there's any doubt, test it by yanking outward and see what happens.

The Stopper placement is flush in this endwise configuration, but how strong is that flake of rock on the right wall of the crack? Probably strong enough to hang off, but not strong enough to hold a leader on a 30-foot ripper. Believe it: The principal cause of anchor failure is rock failure. Protection devices seldom break, but they often rip out, meaning *security,* not strength, is often the main issue.

Both the ball nut and removable bolt are based upon this concept (opposition). While this configuration ("stacked" Stoppers) *will* work, it is rarely used. In this case these two Stoppers mate together rather well, and both have flush contact with each other and the wall of the crack.

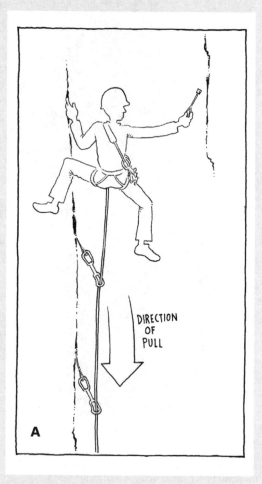

DIRECTION
OF
PULL

A

The direction of pull on protection changes with the next placement. In figure A, the falling climber will impact the protection straight down.

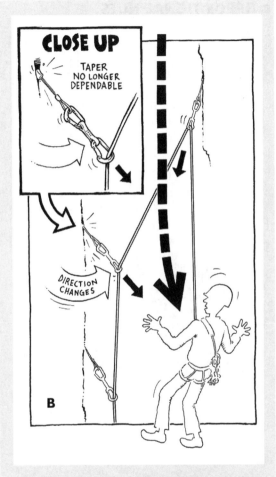

CLOSE UP

TAPER NO LONGER DEPENDABLE

DIRECTION CHANGES

B

Figure B shows how a fall on protection placed higher and out of a direct line with pieces below will change the direction of pull. Note that the falling climber will not pull straight down on the top piece because of the placement of the previous nut.

■ OPPOSITIONAL NUTS

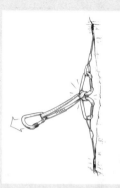

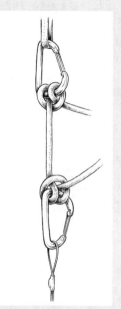

Nuts in opposition, tied together with a clove hitch on a sling, can help solve the direction-of-pull dilemma, especially when an SLCD placement is not available. See the knots chapter for a detailed description of how to tie a clove hitch. This configuration will also work for nuts opposed in a horizontal crack.

A clove hitch can also be used this way to tie off oppositional nuts with a piece of cord or webbing.

Here, clove hitches have been tied directly into the two nuts to eliminate undesirable angles of pull on the placements. Not only do the clove hitches allow the sling to maintain an optimum angle of pull on the nuts, but so long as some pressure is placed on the anchor, inward forces between the pieces keep each nut well set. This is one of the best ways to rig two opposing wired nuts in a horizontal crack, a rare scenario but not unheard of on trad climbs.

■ MICRO-TAPERS (MICRO-NUTS)

TIPS FOR USING MICRO-NUTS:

The clearances of every micro are quite small, so only ideal placements are secure.

Owing to the small surface area, micros are reliable only in good rock.

Lateral forces easily pivot micros out of cracks; always slot the micro directly in the line of pull. This also prevents tweaking the cable.

Always extend the placement with a quickdraw. Rope drag can easily displace the micro.

Avoid placements where the wire is running over an edge.

Avoid jerking the micro too hard, either when setting or removing it, lest you prematurely bend, weaken or even break the wire.

Looking sketchy there . . . This number 6 Micro Stopper (8 kN or 1,798 lbf) has honorable contact on its left side, but the right side is flush only at the base, making the nut very susceptible to displacement by outward force. Placed like this, the taper cannot be relied on to hold anywhere near its rated strength. A slightly smaller nut might better fit in the bottleneck. If this is all you have, set the nut well with several sharp, downward tugs, bearing in mind you have something on the marginal side, untrustworthy for critical situations—like holding a leader fall.

Whenever you have a choice between two equally secure placements, go with the bigger nut as its component strength is higher. But also understand that the quality of both the rock and the placement are typically what make the nut secure/insecure, not the strength of the cable.

Because of micros' boxy shape, near parallel-sided cracks often afford the best placements. Careful placement is essential, because the relative differences between a good and bad micro are small indeed. While it is tempting to slot the nut deep in the crack, it's usually better to keep it where you can visually assess the placement. The right edge of this micro appears to make good contact with the rock, but it's difficult to see exactly what is happening on the left edge. It's troublesome to accurately assess many placements without getting your nose right in there and checking it out.

This Black Diamond Micro Stopper has great surface contact on the left side, almost 100 percent flush, and this is what you're looking for. The right side is also nearly flush, plus the nut simply fits the slot. To secure truly bomber placements, scan the crack for the "V-slot" configuration, and place the nut that best fits the slot. Remember to set the placement with several downward tugs, and give it a test by yanking slightly out and up. A poorly seated nut may hold a ton with a straight, downward load, but may be yanked up and out with a minimal force (like rope drag). Review the breaking strengths of the nuts you buy, and take this into consideration when building your anchor. This number 3 Micro Stopper has a breaking strength of 5 kN (1,123 lbf), compared to a number 6 Stopper (10 kN or 2,248 lbf).

■ ALL THE REST

Hexes

This is what to look for: great surface contact on both sides, with the curve of the nut form-fitting the slot in the rock. Bomber!

Bomber. Great surface contact. A load on this nut would create a camming effect to further key it into the crack.

You couldn't hang your hat on this dud—a common type of endwise placement with beginners. The right side is flush against the wall of the crack, but look at the left side! *Minimal* surface contact. This nut simply does not correspond to the geometry of the crack and would likely fail if loaded. A little higher and deeper in the crack a bomber placement awaits . . .

Good endwise placement—flush contact on both ends, well seated and bomber. Set it well and you're good to go.

Tricams

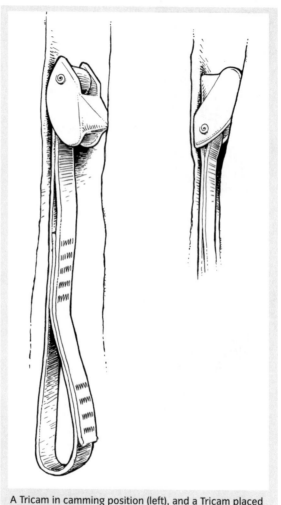

A Tricam in camming position (left), and a Tricam placed as a chock (right).

Big Bros

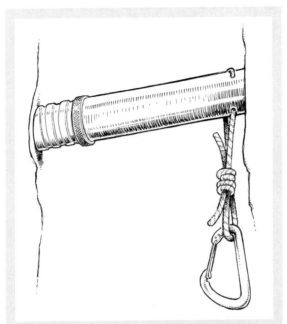

Big Bros, made by Trango, are available in six sizes to fit cracks ranging from 2.7 inches to 18.4 inches wide. A set weighs almost 3½ pounds and costs about $500, but they work like magic—often when nothing else will. With the ends of the Big Bro solidly in contact with the rock (like this), and with the collar tightly cinched, this piece can hold any direction of pull. Big Bros now come color coded for easy size identification.

CHAPTER THREE

Spring-Loaded Camming Devices

THE BASIC ESSENTIALS OF PLACING SLCDs

- Always align the unit with the stem pointing in the anticipated direction of pull.

- To keep the unit from "walking" because of rope drag during a lead, clip a quickdraw into the sewn sling of the unit.

- Try to place the unit near the outside edge of the crack, where you can eyeball the cam lobes to determine their position. This also makes it easier to reach the trigger to clean the device.

- Strive for the ideal placement, with the cams deployed/retracted in the most uniformly parallel section of the crack, so the cams cannot open if the unit walks a bit. Metolius puts color-coded dots on the cams to help with lobe positioning, but with others you'll have to eyeball it. Read and follow the manufacturer's recommendations for cam deployment.

- Use a larger device over a smaller one, but, unless you are absolutely desperate, never force too big a unit into too small a hole. Once the cams are rolled to minimum width, removal, if possible, is grievous.

- Never trust a placement where the cams are nearly "tipped" (the cam lobes almost fully deployed). In such a position there is little room for further expansion, and stability is poor.

(continued)

- Never place a rigid-stemmed unit so the stem is over a lip. A fall can either bend or break the unit. If no other placement is available, tie the unit off short (near the lip of the crack) with a loop of cord.

- Take some time to experiment with marginal placements on the ground. Clip a sling into the SLCD and apply body weight to discover just how far you can trust it. But remember—body weight testing is far milder than a lead fall!

This BD Camalot fits this pocket like a pea in a pod. All four cams have magnificent, flush surface contact, and the range of retraction is about 50 percent. To maximize the holding power of the unit, look for each of the cams to contact the rock at lower to mid expansion range (50 to 90 percent *retracted* for Camalots). All cams are a little different, so be sure to read the manufacturer's guidelines on placement for whatever brand you buy.

green=go

yellow=
caution

red=stop

Camming devices should be placed in the tighter aspect of their range. This flexible-stemmed Metolius unit has colored dots (drilled holes) on the rim of the cams; this placement sits on the borderline between the yellow (caution) and green (go) dots. Remember, *tighter* is better (although leave the last 10 to 25 percent of retraction for removal). The ideal placement is often when the bottom tips of the cams are in line with each other.

Incorrect use of a rigid-stemmed Friend in a horizontal placement risks shearing the stem. This could be improved by tying the unit off short with some cord, right near the lip of the crack.

The best option on a horizontal cam placement is to go with a flexible-stemmed unit. It can withstand a downward bend.

This Camalot is retracted only about 10 percent. Based on the "constant camming angle" (engineers call it the logarithmic spiral), a camming device will theoretically work at any point in the range. Throughout the cam's rotation, a line drawn from the axle to the cam's point of contact (with the wall of the crack) will remain at the same angle to a line drawn perpendicular from the stem. However, the most secure placements will be those in the lower to mid expansion range (50 to 90 percent retracted). Try to shoot

for placements where the bottom tips of all four cams come into line. With all camming devices, tighter is better, though if you don't leave at least 10 to 25 percent off the tightest retraction position, you'll likely never get the unit out.

Here a larger camming device is called for. And if this is all you've got—beware. If loaded directly downward, the unit may be strong. But this unit lacks stability and security, as the cams are not adequately supported, and the unit could possibly twist out of the placement and fail.

Also beware of the walking phenomenon. The action of a rope wiggling through a carabiner (or the repeated falling or lowering of someone on a toprope) can force a placement like this to pivot back and forth and "walk" upward. If the crack is wider above the placement, the cams can possibly open even further, rendering the placement worthless. A long sling can help prevent this, but not eliminate the possibility altogether. Avoid situations where the camming device may walk into a wider section of the crack, and look for that sweet, tightly retracted placement, ideally in a pod or a crack with parallel-sided walls.

This Camalot is retracted about 50 percent. Think of 50 percent as a starting point—shoot for 50 percent or tighter. This placement could be improved simply by placing it slightly higher and deeper in the crack. Avoid placing camming devices on the edge of a crack (particularly in soft rock like sandstone), and look for placements in the most parallel-sided spot in the crack, avoiding any flares like the one directly below this placement.

This Camalot placement has several problems. While the rock looks sound, the outer cam on the left wall of the crack is too close to the edge. The real problem, however, is the violation of this rule, listed in the Black Diamond literature under BAD PLACEMENTS: "Never place a unit so that the cams are offset, e.g., with two cams extended and two cams retracted. It may not hold a fall."

Strive to keep the loading axis (the axle) near the middle. That is, when the SLCD is placed, it forms a shape, and you want the axle to be pretty much dead center in that shape. If the axle is too far to one side or the other of the cam lobes, the physics are all wrong and the loading is unstable.

This old-style rigid-stemmed Friend is too small for the crack, obvious because the two lobes on the right side are "tipped out." As mentioned, when the lobes are at or near the limit of their possible breadth, the unit is considered marginal. Even the slightest rope drag can pivot the piece enough for the lobe to invert, like a sprung umbrella, rendering the unit worthless. Often you can jockey the unit around and find a better placement. If not, use a bigger unit. Fact is, you climb long enough and you'll inevitably have to make just such a placement. The crack will be just this size, and the only unit left on your rack will be too small. Place it, trying to find the narrowest place in the crack. It may hold. But understand that you are hoping the unit performs beyond the specs for which it was designed.

Here the rock is solid and the placement looks bomber. But the gate on the biner is contacting the rock and could possibly open when loaded. Remember that when a carabiner is loaded with the gate open, it loses two-thirds of its strength. By looping a sling through the SLCD using the "basket" configuration (see below), this problem is easily remedied.

Solution to above problem.

This Camalot is placed in the middle of its expansion range, but the crack widens appreciably just above the unit. A little rope wiggle could walk the piece up into the opening, rendering it useless. A taper or hex would fit better in a crack that constricts like this, whereas this camming unit would be better placed in a more parallel section.

This crack is too small for this cam, which is placed with the cams cranked to minimum width. Removal might be difficult. Avoid such placements if at all possible, although in dire circumstances with no other options, it is better to risk losing a cam than losing your life.

CHAPTER FOUR

Bolts

The ubiquitous hex-head 5-piece Rawl bolt. Somewhat of a standard, this is probably the most common bolt you'll encounter, now sold under the brand name Powers Bolt. In a good placement the hanger should snug up flush and flat against the wall. A 5-piece Rawl actually has 6 pieces. In solid granite the ⅜-inch diameter rates at over 7,000 pounds shear strength and almost 5,000 pounds pullout strength.

Behold the woeful "spinner." This buttonhead bolt protrudes from the hole and the hanger is not flush against the rock. The hole was not drilled deep enough, and when hammered in, the shaft bottomed out in the back of the hole, preventing the head of the bolt from pinning the hanger flush against the rock.

A relic from the old days, this ¼-inch Rawl Drive buttonhead still looks good after twenty-five years; the stainless steel hanger shows no signs of corrosion. In trad climbing areas most aging, ¼-inch bolts have been replaced, but you'll still find some on more obscure climbs, stuck in the stone like slow-ticking time bombs. In fine-grained, iron-hard granite, one of these contraction bolts *might* hold 2,000 pounds. In anything less than perfect rock, old Rawl buttonheads should never be trusted. Here the placement looks acceptable: The bolt is perpendicular to the plane of the rock face, and the head of the bolt and hanger is flush to the rock. What can't be judged by visual inspection is the length of the bolt. These ¼ buttonheads come in lengths ranging from ¾ inch to 1½ inches. I've replaced dozens of these ¼-inch bolts over the years. Many were removed simply by putting a claw hammer behind the hanger and prying outward, with about the same force required to pull a nail from a piece of particleboard.

Amazingly, this bolt shows virtually no signs of corrosion after thirty years at Joshua Tree. Stainless steel has become the standard for bolts and hangers as it protects against corrosion, although many carbon steel bolts are used because they are less expensive.

This ⅜-inch threaded Rawl bolt looks perfectly set in great rock—good to go.

WHAT TO DO WITH THAT BOLT . . .

There is no absolutely reliable method to test in-situ bolts, but there are plenty of reasons to want to. Here are some suggestions:

Always consider a ¼-inch bolt suspect. They haven't been placed as anchors for over two decades, though they are still found on older routes.

Make sure the bolt hanger is flush to the wall and not a "spinner," where the hanger spins freely on the stud. A spinner indicates the hole was drilled too shallow for the bolt stud, or that the bolt stud has crept out from the hole, which happens with contraction bolts. And don't try to fix the spinner by hammering on it. Had that been possible, the first party would have sunk it. Further hammering can only damage the shank and the head.

Keep an eye out for cratering, which occurs in brittle or extremely hard rock, and is usually the result of sloppy drilling, which forms a chipped-away crater around the hole.

(continued)

- Check the hanger for cracks.

- If the bolt is a screwhead, make sure the nut is snug and the threads are in good shape. I learned this after taking a 30-foot grounder (into a snowbank, luckily) when the hanger popped off the denuded threads of such a bolt. If the bolt is a buttonhead, or looks like a machine bolt, again make sure it's snugly set and free of fatigue cracks.

- If the bolt is clearly bent, or looks to be set in an oblique hole, beware!

- Discoloration is natural enough, but excessive rust denotes a so-called coffin nail. Use common sense. If the bolt looks funky, don't trust it. And always back up bolts (that don't meet the modern standard) with a nut, if possible. A perfect bolt is nearly impossible to pull out, even with an astronomical fall, but there are a lot of bolts out there that are something less than perfect. Better safe than splattered.

These hangers were recalled long ago by Ed Leeper due to stress corrosion problems. Though unreliable, many such hangers are still out there, especially in classic trad areas. These hangers should be replaced and upgraded to stainless steel, as should all ¼-inch bolts.

Bolt Hangers

This ¼-inch buttonhead is installed using the infamous "SMC Death Hanger," a moniker that stuck after several such hangers failed under body weight (possibly due to a stress corrosion problem) on Yosemite's Middle Cathedral Rock. The hanger has taken on a distinctly bronze tint. It is roughly as thick as a quarter, much thinner than the more recent SMC hanger below. NOT to be trusted.

While over twenty years old, this threaded Rawl bolt and stainless steel SMC hanger still look good. The rock is solid desert granite, the placement is perpendicular and the hanger is flush. Every twenty-year-old bolt should look so good.

A ⅜-inch 5-piece Rawl with a Metolius hanger. Somebody painted it to match the rock, but the paint is chipping off. Factory-painted bolts fare much better.

This welded steel cold shut shows signs of corrosion just a few years after installation. Many manufacturers (such as FIXE) now offer the preferable stainless steel cold shuts. While more expensive, they'll most likely last a lifetime.

CHAPTER FIVE

Fall Forces

FORCES FACTS

- Essential peak (dynamic) force load-limiter qualities in the belay system depend on flex and give in the components.

- Flex and give in the belay system keep dynamic forces of a real world factor 2 fall lower than forces recorded in the lab during a "simulated factor 2 fall drop test."

- The top piece always absorbs the greatest force during a fall, therefore *the top piece is the most important component in the entire belay chain—* be it a point of protection, or the belay anchor itself.

- Make certain, so far as humanly possible, that the top piece of pro, and not the belay anchor, arrests any and all leader falls.

- The main task of the belay is to limit loading on the topmost protection.

- The most critical time is when a leader is first leaving the belay and has yet to place the first piece of protection.

- The belay anchor is not completed, and the roped safety system is not truly on-line, till a secure piece of protection is placed.

This shows a climber running the lead rope through the anchor points as he takes off on lead. If he should fall, his full weight will come onto the anchor, not the belayer, which is a mixed blessing. It might mean less force directly on the belayer, but it will double the forces on the anchor. Better for this climber to forego running the rope through the anchor and instead place a bomber piece of protection as soon as possible, probably from his current stance, where the crack looks willing to accept a good piece.

Climbers on the extremely runout *Bachar-Yerian* route in Toulumne. Notice how the first bolt placed by the leader is only a few feet above the belay—this will help absorb the force of a fall rather than having all that force put directly on the anchor. The sooner you can put in that first bomber piece, the better. If you're placing natural gear, an SLCD works well because of its multidirectional capabilities.

CHAPTER SIX

Judging the Direction of Pull

DIRECTION OF PULL

Every fall generates a dynamic force that will *pull* on the roped safety system from a specific *direction or directions.*

The direction of pull is described by a direct line between the belayer and the first piece (when belaying a leader) of pro, or the last piece of pro (when belaying a follower) through which the rope runs.

Lead protection and belay anchors must sustain loading from every direction of pull that is possible on a specific pitch.

To accurately judge the direction of pull, you must know where the route goes.

When the direction of pull is uncertain, a multidirectional belay anchor is required.

When a swinging fall directly onto protection, or onto the belay anchor, is possible, the pro and the belay anchor must be built to sustain loading across the full arc of the swing.

Knowing the direction of pull is to a climber what knowing the direction of a possible ambush is to a foot soldier: *essential for survival.*

The climber following this pitch is unclipping the last piece. As long as that piece is still clipped, the direction of pull on the belayer and anchor in the event of a fall will be in a straight line toward that last piece. However, when the piece is unclipped, the direction of pull will be in an arc below the belayer, and the anchor better be built to withstand the swinging load. It's no problem with this bolted belay, but hand-built anchors require careful thought. PHOTO BY STEWART M. GREEN.

This leader has traversed left off the belay, and if she falls
before clipping that first piece, the load on the anchor will
describe an approximately 90-degree arc below the belayer.
If the anchor is built to withstand only a straight up or down
pull, this could spell trouble. PHOTO BY STEWART M. GREEN.

CHAPTER SEVEN

Knots for Anchoring

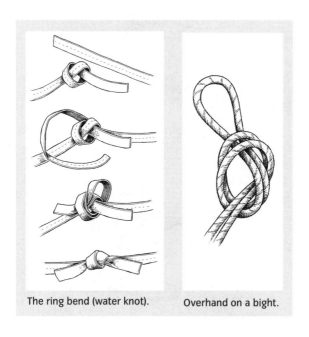

The ring bend (water knot).

Overhand on a bight.

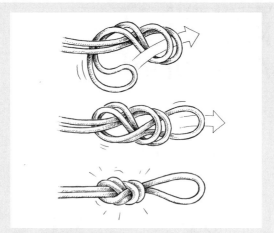

Figure eight on a bight.

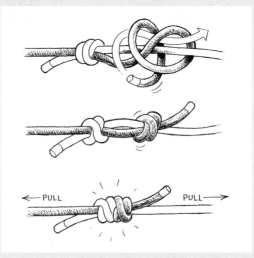

Double fisherman's knot. Add one more loop around each end to make a triple fisherman's knot.

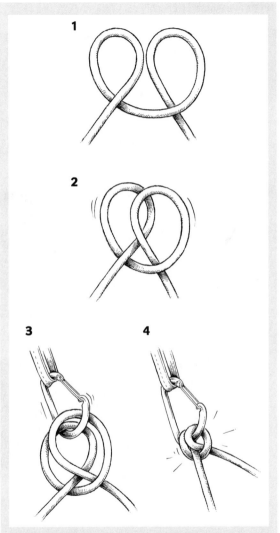

1

2

3

4

Clove hitch. The rope going straight down from the biner in the final illustration is the load strand.

How to tie a bowline-on-a-bight.

1

2

3

4

5

The bowline-on-a-bight is useful for anchoring with the rope to a two-point anchor system, such as two bolts at a hanging belay. It can also be used to equalize two points of a multicomponent gear anchor, although other systems presented later in this book are superior.

The Munter hitch.

1. Twist rope.

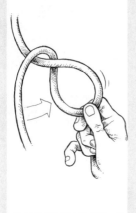

2. Hold in place.

3. Clip as shown.

4. Pull up and out. In this example, the belayer's brake hand is placed on the strand going down right. The upward strand goes to the climber.

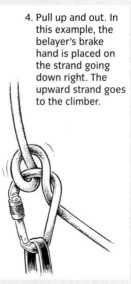

ANCHOR SYSTEMS

CHAPTER EIGHT

Belay Anchors

CLIFF NOTES ON REDUNDANCY

- Redundancy Credo: *Never trust a single piece of gear.*

- Proper redundancy ensures that if any one component fails, the anchor will not automatically fail.

- Redundancy asks that anchor systems be constructed of multiple components—from the primary placements, to the slings and biners used for connecting placements.

- According to NASA, *doubling-up (making redundant) components within any system greatly increases their reliability* (over single component setups). Tripling slightly increases reliability over doubled setups. Quadrupling makes practically no difference.

(continued)

In real world climbing you sometimes cannot make redundant every facet of the system, but there is every reason to try.

A fail-safe anchor, not redundancy per se, is the ultimate goal, and redundancy is only one important tool to achieve that goal.

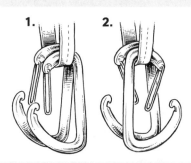

Doubled carabiners should always have the gates opposite and opposed. Locking carabiners would provide even more security.

1. The wrong way. Even if one of the carabiners is flipped over so the gates are on opposite sides, the gates are still not technically opposed.

2. The right way. Even if one of the biners flipped over and the gates were on the same side, the direction they open would still be in opposition.

SRENE Anchors

- Solid
- Equalized
- Redundant
- No Extension

KEY SRENE POINTS

SRENE is an evaluation strategy, not a checklist.

Observance of every SRENE principle does not guarantee that an anchor will hold a single pound.

Modern rigging techniques cannot compensate for insecure primary placements.

With strong primary placements and modern rigging techniques providing security, climbing's roped safety system is typically very reliable.

STEP-BY-STEP BELAY ANCHOR

On popular routes the belay stances/ledges are usually well established (though not always ideal). Belay there.

Further narrow your belay site down to the most secure, ergonomic and practical position.

Locate suitable cracks or rock features to fashion a "good enough" belay anchor.

Set the most bombproof, primary big nut or camming device you can find—preferably a multidirectional placement—and tie yourself off before yelling "off belay."

Determine the direction(s) of pull for both the climber following the pitch and the leader casting off on the next lead.

(continued)

Simply and efficiently shore up the primary placement with secondary anchors.

Try to set the secondary placements in close, but not cramped, proximity.

If the rock is less than perfect in quality, spread the anchors out, using several features, to preserve redundancy.

Using modern rigging techniques, connect the various components of the system together so they function as one unit to safeguard against all possible directions of pull.

Consider tying into the most bombproof anchor with a clove hitch (to aid adjustability).

When bringing up a second after leading a pitch, if possible situate your body in line between the anchors and the anticipated direction of pull. Remember ABC: Anchor——➤ Belayer——➤ Climber.

Also remember KISS: Keep It Simple, Stupid. Avoid overbuilding.

This photo shows decent technique for tying into an anchor the old-fashioned way, directly with a rope, which might be necessary if you're short on gear or in some sort of emergency situation. An SLCD and hexentric are tied off tight with clove hitches to a backup SLCD above. The lower SLCD is set as an oppositional piece to hold an upward pull. The belayer is tied into the strand of the rope coming down on the left side of the photo, which will minimize extension if the lowest piece fails. Note that the load strands of the clove hitches are cinched nice and tight, with no strands on the gate of the biner. You might consider belaying the second through a biner connected to one of the upper pieces, especially if you're expecting someone to struggle and hang on the rope.

■ CORDELETTES

A STANDARD CORDELETTE:

Is a statically equalized system that is most effective when its arms are of equal length.

Normally consists of an 18-foot piece of 7mm nylon
cord (tied into a loop with a double fisherman's
knot) or 5.5mm high-tensile cord (connected with a
triple fisherman's knot).

TO RIG A CORDELETTE:

Clip the cordelette into the primary anchors, then
pull the loops of cord down between each of the
pieces.

Pull the arms of the cordelette tight toward the
anticipated loading direction (direction of pull).

Align the fisherman's knot so it is below the highest primary placement in the system, free and
clear of the power point knot.

Secure the power point with an overhand knot or,
if you have enough cord, a figure eight knot. Tie
the power point loop about 4 inches in diameter,
roughly the same size as the belay loop on your
harness.

Clip into the power point with a section of the
climbing rope, not with a daisy chain or other
device made of high-tensile cord.

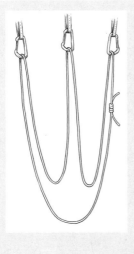

The cordelette attaches multiple anchor points with a single, mostly static tie-in point. Remember to keep the fisherman's knot up out of the way like this. With equal-length arms and a predictable direction of pull (straight up or down), a cordelette like this is a viable anchor choice.

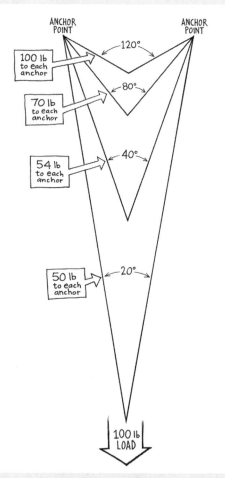

How a 100-pound load is distributed between two anchors rigged at various angles. Whether rigging with a cordelette, equalette or sliding X, the forces on the primary placements increase significantly at greater angles.

Belay anchor with three SLCDs tied off with a cordelette.
The granite is sound, and all three cams are bomber, well
retracted (over 50 percent), with all the cams nicely contacting the walls of the crack. The rope is attached to the power
point with two carabiners opposed and reversed (including
one locking). Clean, simple and strong. The bottom cam
means this anchor could also withstand an upward force.

Note that load equalization over placements set in a
vertical crack is much more a concept than a fact. Here the
bulk of direct, downward loading will fall on the middle
SLCD.

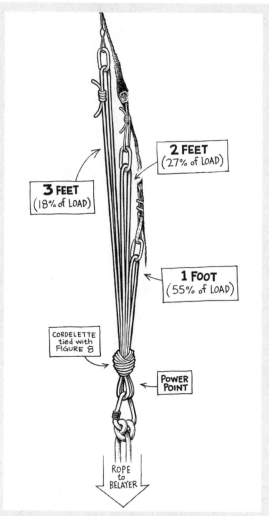

2 FEET
(27% of LOAD)

3 FEET
(18% of LOAD)

1 FOOT
(55% of LOAD)

CORDELETTE
tied with
FIGURE 8

POWER
POINT

ROPE
to
BELAYER

Using a cordelette to connect anchors in a vertical crack results in an anchor that does not come close to truly equalizing the forces.

Four camming devices in a horizontal crack connected with a cordelette. Note how the fisherman's knot (on the cordelette) is rigged well out of the way. As with all statically equalized anchors, the setup is set for a single direction of pull. Even the slightest oblique angle of pull will load one side of the triangle while the other side will bear little if any load. Stretchy nylon cord is more forgiving in this regard, but off-axis loading will still weight one of the placements over the others. However, because the arms of the cordelette are of equal length here, climbers can expect to achieve some equalization as long as the direction of pull is straight down.

This cordelette has been unknotted and used in the "Web-o-lette" mode. This is a trick adopted by many professional guides to add greater utility to their cordelette. When untied, the cord works well for connecting three points when a standard cordelette, describing a single loop, would be too short. Simply tie the ends with figure eights, clip into the two outside anchor points in a V configuration, take the middle bight and clip it into a third point. Then gather the two bights together and tie a two-loop power point with a figure eight.

In this particular setup, all three camming devices are bomber, and the granite is sound. Notice the upper left camming device has a sling looped through in the "basket" mode, to prevent the carabiner from grinding on the edge of the crack. The lower left camming device has a locking carabiner to prevent the gate opening on the crack edge, and a slight improvement here would be to do the same at the upper right cam. While there is some loss of strength in those arms of the cordelette with a single strand, this rig—based on bomber primary placements—is a trade-off most climbers can live with.

As is always the case with such setups, this is rigged for a downward pull, and any oblique loading will put the load on one of the other three primary placements. Also, because the arms of the cordelette are of unequal length, true equalization is not achieved.

■ THE SLIDING X

SLIDING X BASICS:

■ The sliding X is an automatic equalizing system.

■ It is normally rigged on standard length and/or double-length sewn slings.

■ A proper twist in the sliding X sling is essential to prevent failure of the complete system if one piece pulls. Always double-check to be sure that this twist is in place.

■ After connecting the sliding X to the placements, clip a biner into the X, weight the placements and slide the biner back and forth along the sling to ensure fluid functioning.

■ To minimize potential extension in longer equaliz-ing slings, tie an overhand limiter knot in the long leg of the sling, just above the tie-in point.

■ To avoid load multiplication, keep the angle between the two legs around 25 degrees (or less). If the angle is larger than about 45 degrees, use a longer sling to decrease the angle.

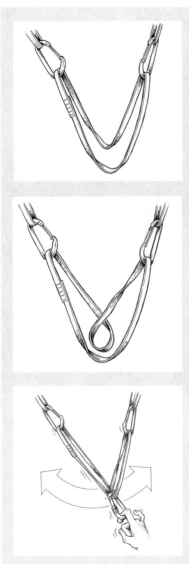

The sliding X equalizes an anchor dynamically when the load changes directions.

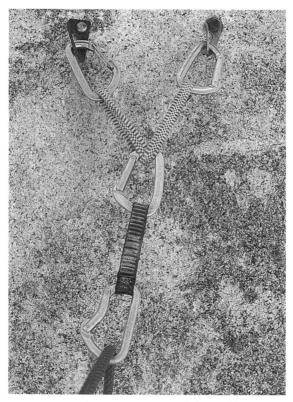

A sliding X connecting two bolts. This self-equalizing technique can be used when leading if the need arises to spread potential loading over two sketchy bolts placed close together, or two marginal pieces of gear.

A three-piece anchor equalized with sliding X's. The lower sling has been doubled to adjust the location of the power point.

Here we have a pre-equalized anchor, meaning no self-equalizing sliding X is used on the right-hand placement. That sling has been shortened and pre-equalized by tying a limiter knot. This anchor is rigged for a downward pull only. The equalization looks tight, and even though it's impossible to achieve the best equalization with such a static system, this anchor could easily hold two tons. Once loaded, however, even under body weight, those thin slings will be *very* difficult to unknot, particularly at the overhand knots.

Here we have the same anchor as shown on the previous page, except now the three pieces are self-equalized with two sliding X knots. Unlike the previous anchor, if the load angle changes on this setup, the anchor will remain equalized. The limiter knot tied into the right-hand sling just above the power point will limit extension if the right piece should fail. However, the knot also serves to limit the equalization potential of this anchor—as with every setup, compromises are part of the deal.

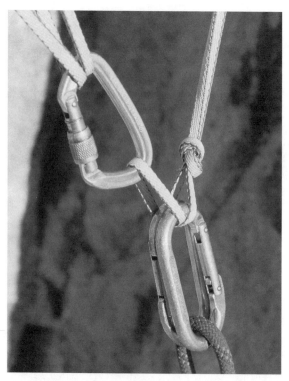

Close-up of previous photo. An overhand limiter knot is tied on the right side of the sliding knot to check extension if the piece should fail.

Three camming devices equalized with a sliding X and clove hitches. This is a good belay anchor rig for a multipitch climb, providing the two climbers are swinging leads. Since there is no power point, climbers swapping leads at this belay stance will require the arriving climber to also rig his rope in this fashion. No big deal, but a bit more time consuming, and a real cluster if there were a third climber at this stance. If one of the two CDs on top were to blow out, there would be sudden loading on the remaining anchor; but judging by the placements (A-1), this would be nearly impossible, even in a factor 2 fall situation, as the downward force would be shared by the two cams, and the force required to break the sling would be astronomical.

Opposite: Same anchor as on page 77, now rigged to be entirely self-equalizing. An overhand limiter knot tied on the left side of the upper sling (configured in a sliding X) would limit extension if the top cam failed. This rig, in turn, is equalized with two slings paired up and attached (via a sliding X) to the lower piece, to safeguard against an upward/outward pull on the anchor.

Deceptively clean, simple and effective, it normally takes a leader some time to A) survey a given belay and quickly decide upon such a system, and B) quickly and efficiently rig same. While its utility has been proven over several decades, initial work with the sliding X is sometimes confusing. Ultimately there are but a few tricks to using the sliding X, including the limiter knots to reduce extension. Much of the process is simplified once you can quickly determine what size slings are needed for a given setup, as well as your ability to shorten the slings as needed. Using, or trying to use, oversize slings—which adds needless slack in the system—is a common error when first employing the sliding X. As with all anchor building, confidence and efficiency comes with practice.

■ THE EQUALETTE

TYING THE EQUALETTE:

Use 20 feet of 7mm nylon cord tied into a loop with a double fisherman's knot, or 5mm high-tensile cord tied with a triple fisherman's knot.

Form a U shape and grab the cordelette at the bottom of the U.

Position the fisherman's knot about 18 inches above the bottom of the U.

Tie an overhand knot on each side of your palm where you have grabbed the cord, about 10 inches apart.

USING THE EQUALETTE:

At the power point, always use two locking biners, with one locker connected into each separate strand of the power point (between the limiter knots). If you are forced to use one biner, clip one strand, twist the other 180 degrees, then clip the other strand to maintain redundancy. This is the same technique used to clip into a sliding X.

Before using the equalette, make sure you have mastered the clove hitch. Use clove hitches to adjust the arm lengths, as shown in the photos.

On multipitch climbs (with a two-climber team) where the first climber to the stance is going to lead the next pitch, each climber can clip into the power point with his own two locking biners. If the second climber to the stance is going to lead the next pitch, he can clip a locking biner directly into the two-locking-biner power point (biner to biner). This greatly facilitates secure and speedy turnover at the belay.

This closeup of an equalette power point (tied using slings rather than cord) clearly shows how to rig two locking bin-ers through the strands between the limiter knots. The belayer is tied into the power point with a figure eight knot. This setup will remain equalized if the load swings right or left, but if one anchor should fail, the limiter knots will mini-mize extension in the system.

Three-piece anchor rigged with an equalette. Not only solidly equalized but able to adjust to changes in loading direction. The right arm of the anchor is tied off to two pieces and adjusted with clove hitches. The left arm has been shortened with a figure eight on a bight.

Three-piece anchor rigged with an equalette.

Four-piece equalette rig. Very simple and very stout.

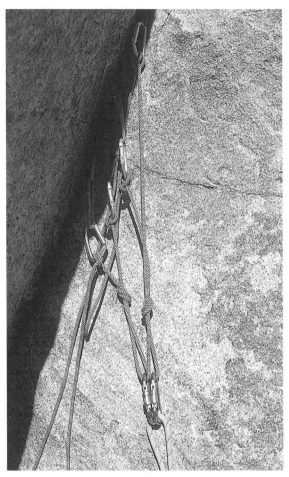

A four-piece equalette rig. Four placements in a vertical crack usually result in a complicated and messy rigging system. Here everything is simple and clean, with good equalization between the two arms and some load sharing between the strands of each arm. While it is unrealistic to think any rigging system can equally load four placements, this equalette comes as close as you will likely get when using a single sling to connect four placements.

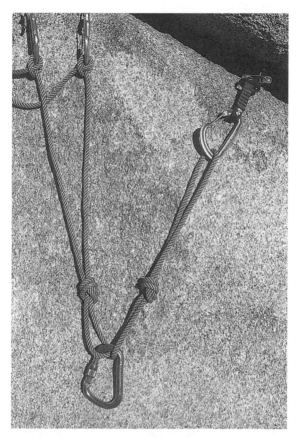

Three-piece anchor connected with an equalette. This system is clean, simple and well equalized. When only using one locking biner at the power point, clip it through one strand, then twist the other strand 180 degrees and clip into it. The technique is the same as clipping into a sling to form a sliding X.

The Quad

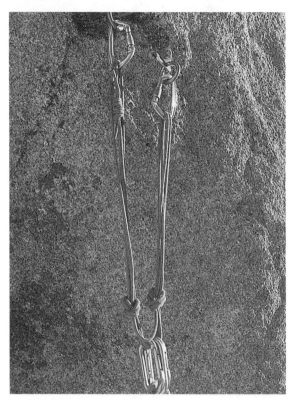

Two-bolt "quad" rig for toprope setup. The quad is simply a doubled equalette. Lab testing suggests that for two horizontally oriented anchor points (as shown here), the quad setup is basically indestructible. Field testing suggests that for those who frequently belay from, or toprope off, two horizontally oriented bolts (as found on top of countless sport and toprope climbs), a quad rig is your best friend. Simply keep it rigged (with the limiter knots tied) on a piece of 7mm nylon or 5mm high-strength cord and break it out for use in these situations. Brute strength and fantastic equalization are achieved just as quickly as you can clip off the bolts and the power point.

Quad rig close-up. At 5,000-pound test for each strand, clip-ping just two strands at the power point gives you twice the strength ever needed. Clip three and have a submarine anchor.

■ COMPOSITE ANCHORS: CORDELETTE, SLIDING X AND EQUALETTE

Multipitch anchor with cordelette and sliding X combo. While this setup—and ones like it—have been a mainstay for many years, incorporating new techniques such as the equalette will allow climbers to achieve even greater equal-ization.

■ UPWARD OPPOSITIONAL ANCHORS

UPWARD FORCE OPPOSITIONALS ARE REQUIRED:

☐ When a belayer is significantly lighter than the active climber.

☐ Whenever belaying below an overhang and the initial protection off the belay anchor is directly above or even behind (such as with a roof crack) the anchor.

☐ Where the rock is steep or overhanging and the forces generated by a leader fall can create significant (say, more than 18 inches) "lift" of the belayer.

This rig shows a cordelette used to equalize the load on two tapers with another SLCD placed to provide opposition. A belayer tied tight to these anchors isn't going to be lifted any more than 18 inches— enough to provide some "give" in the system, but not enough to be dangerous.

■ BELAY POSITIONS

Here the belay device is clipped into the belay loop on the climber's harness—an **indirect belay.** Providing the belayer has a solid stance to brace against downward loading, the indirect belay is the technique of choice if the anchor is less than superb. In holding a fall, the belayer bears the brunt of the fall force, which can be uncomfortable and awkward when the falling climber hangs on the rope for a long period of time.

Though this setup is adequate for the low-angled slab it is servicing, if the terrain below was vertical (meaning higher loading), the belayer's backside might get dragged down to a position directly below the anchor. Remember that when the system is loaded, gravity pulls every object on the rope into the fall line, into a position directly below the anchor. Here we have a classic trade-off: In terms of managing forces, the best position for the belayer is directly below the anchor, where downward loading can only pull him straight down. But here the best body position is slightly to the left of the anchor—meaning his arse and brisket will have to bear the bulk of the loading. If the loading becomes greater than what he can maintain (very unlikely on this slab toprope setup), downward loading will pull him down and across to where he is directly beneath the anchor.

Though not always possible, the ideal is: With any indirect belay, the belayer should try to get into a position directly beneath the belay anchor to avoid getting dragged there by downward loading. Remember ABC positioning for bringing up the second: Anchor ⟶ Belayer ⟶ Climber.

Here the belay device is clipped into both the harness's belay loop *and* the loop in the figure eight tie-in knot. If the climber falls, most of his weight goes onto the anchor, *not* on the belayer—providing that the belayer is situated directly beneath the anchor. To the extent that the belayer is to one side or the other of the anchor is the extent that his body, not the anchor, will bear the load.

This shows how a **re-directed belay** is set up. Always remember that a re-direct basically doubles the loading on the anchor—no problem with premium anchors (like bolts on a sport climb), but with sketchy anchors, a re-directed belay is a little dicey.

This effectively illustrates a clean and simple rigging of a **direct belay**. Whenever the primary placements in the anchor matrix are stout, many climbers find this setup the most user friendly, especially when the second is slip-sliding and hanging all over the route. Under these circumstances, it's almost always better that the anchor (providing it is bomber) bears the loading, not the belayer's corpus.

A three-bolt anchor rigged for a **direct belay** (direct belay = belaying directly off the belay anchor) via a Petzl Grigri clipped into the power point. Note how the power point is at an ergonomically friendly chest level, ideal for managing a direct belay. Beyond the Grigri, other popular auto-locking devices are the Petzl Reverso, the Black Diamond ATC Guide, and the Trango Cinch. Here, another direct belay option would include the Munter hitch on a large, pear-shaped locking carabiner.

Remember this: A direct belay is an easy and efficient means to belay the second or follower, but never should be used to belay the leader. Also, understand that with all direct belays, when the anchors are less than ideal, any loading bypasses the shock-absorbing qualities of the belayer's body, and places the entire load directly onto the anchors. Granted, toprope forces are generally moderate, but any force is a concern if you've wandered off route and get stuck belaying from mank. When the anchors are rock solid, however, a direct belay is a quick, efficient and comfortable way to bring up a second.

Three-bolt anchor rigged as a **re-directed** belay. Understand that with every re-directed belay, the load is almost doubled where the rope is re-directed through the anchor. Always a sketchy choice when the follower considerably outweighs the belayer; if not well braced for the loading, a sudden force greater than their body weight can slam the belayer into the wall. Re-directed belays add friction to the system. When the belayer is equal to or bigger than the follower and the anchors are mint, this technique makes for smooth and fluid lowering if the second is climbing up to, then getting lowered off, an anchor.

Guides frequently use a rope-direct when the anchor is set back from the edge and they want to position themselves near the edge to eyeball their client. In this setup you run the rope through two biners at the anchor's power point, climb back down to the edge, then tie an overhand loop on the doubled bight of rope. This now serves as an extended power point, and the belayer is secured where he wants to be. Here a Grigri is used for a direct belay from the new power point.

This is an easy technique that is especially useful at one-pitch crags where you belay from the top and the anchors are often set back from the edge. The end of the rope is clipped to the power point of the anchor system with a figure eight on a bight. Find your belay position and tie another figure eight (which becomes an extended power point), then simply secure yourself with a locking biner to your belay loop, and rig a direct belay (with a separate locking biner) off the extended power point.

As always, downward forces will try to drag the belayer into a direct line beneath the anchor—which is exactly where you might end up if your stance is not adequate and the anchor is not directly behind you.

CHAPTER NINE

Other Anchors

■ TOPROPE ANCHORS

TIPS FOR SETTING

Evaluate any hazards at the site, especially loose rocks that the movement of a running rope could dislodge.

Extend the anchors over the edge at the top of the cliff to prevent rope drag and damage. Professional guides prefer to rig this extension with a length of static rope. Pad any sharp edges at the lip. Make sure the rope sits directly above the climb, and make sure to run two independent strands of rope or webbing over the lip to maintain redundancy.

Set the chocks and SLCDs fairly close together near the top of the climb when possible to reduce the number of slings and carabiners required.

Avoid setting pieces behind detached blocks, flakes or other questionable rock features. Also, avoid having the rope near these features.

Connect the rope to the anchors with two opposed carabiners, at least one of which is locking. If a spare locking carabiner isn't available, be sure the gates are opposed, and add a third carabiner.

(continued)

- Belay toprope climbs from the ground whenever possible.

- Avoid belaying directly below the climber, in case rocks come off.

- A ground anchor merely needs to provide extra ballast to help you counterweight the climber, so one bombproof piece is usually sufficient.

- If you're in an exposed situation where getting yanked from your ground belay would be disastrous or even fatal, set up a redundant anchor system.

"Good enough" toprope anchor. The bolts are 5-piece Rawls installed with FIXE ring anchors. The high-tensile cord (4,000 pounds *single-loop strength* with triple fisherman's knot) is doubled then tied with a figure eight, leaving a four-loop power point. The rope is attached with three oval carabiners opposed and reversed. Clean, simple and strong. As discussed earlier, any off-axis loading will put most or all of the force on one bolt, but in this situation it's extremely unlikely the anchor will fail.

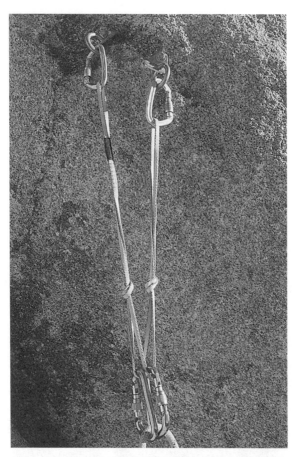

A two-bolt equalette rigged with webbing for an absolutely bomber toprope setup. Note how the gates are opposed and reversed on the carabiners. Owing to the sliding power point, this equalette can remain almost perfectly equalized between the two bolts, even if the direction of pull should change.

The use of a static rope can simplify extending a toprope anchor over the edge of a cliff. Each arm of the "V" is connected to two camming devices, and the power point is a double-loop figure eight. The extension rope is connected to the toprope by three oval carabiners, gates reversed and opposed.

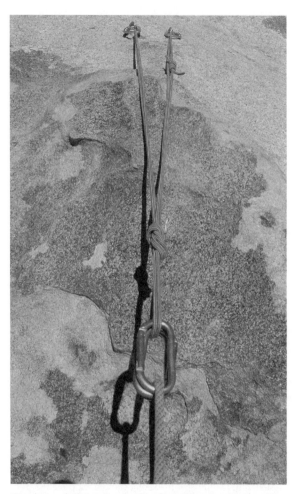

Simple two-bolt toprope anchor featuring a cordelette with two-loop power point. Rope is attached with two oval carabiners, opposed and reversed. The problem here is the way in which the carabiners rest right on an edge. This can cause the gates to open and create a dangerous situation. Always extend your toprope anchor over the lip of any such edges.

This toprope anchor consists of a 7mm nylon cordelette attached to two bolts with locking carabiners, pre-equalized with a figure eight on a bight and an overhand. The rope is attached with three ovals, opposed and reversed. The rope runs cleanly on this rig due to the fact that the power point has been extended beyond the lip. An extra figure eight knot has been added to shorten the rig and situate the power point exactly where desired.

Clean and straightforward use of a static rope to extend a
TR anchor over the edge. Both ends of the "V" have two
camming devices statically equalized with cordelettes, tied
with a figure eight on a bight on the left side and a clove
hitch on the right side (for easy adjustability for the final
equalization).

The primary placements are solid, secure and well equalized, but why not tie a limiter knot near the power point to limit extension? If you can determine the exact direction of pull/loading—and normally you can on any toprope setup—there is little to gain by using the sliding X. And in this case there's no redundancy at the webbing. All this anchor needs is a limiter knot at the power point and then you'd have it: Solid, Redundant, Equalized, and No Extension.

Same TR anchor as in the previous photo, but here the anchors are tied off with pre-equalized slings and joined with a cordelette. Providing the direction of pull is straight down—and it is on this toprope route—such a setup is superior to the setup in the previous photo, with its sliding X. The point is, you need not worry as much about building a multidirectional anchor when the direction of possible loading is only in one direction.

■ RAPPEL ANCHORS

TIPS FOR SETTING

▢ Statistically, rappelling is one of the most dangerous procedures in all of climbing.

▢ Rappelling forces you to rely completely on your equipment and anchors/rigging.

▢ Simple and avoidable rigging failures, not displaced nuts, cams, etc., are statistically the highest cause of rappelling accidents.

▢ Never trust, and always thoroughly check, the integrity of fixed rappel anchors (especially the rigging), and back them up if necessary.

▢ Excepting huge trees and titanic natural features, at least two bombproof anchors should be established at rappel stations.

▢ Avoid the American triangle rigging system. Anchors should be rigged using equalized slings, or at least slings of equal length.

▢ Never run the rope around a chain connecting the anchors.

▢ Double-check all connecting links (anchor placements/slings, slings/rope, rope/rappel device, rappel device/harness) before you start down.

▢ Always rappel slowly and smoothly to keep a low, static load on the anchor.

Two ⅜-inch bolts. The left bolt has a stainless steel hanger, then a steel quick link to a steel lap link through which the rope is threaded. The right bolt has a welded cold shut with chain. The tackle on this anchor is a witless medley of various hardware store fixtures, none of which are designed for climbing anchors. The equalization looks good, and the rope is threaded through two different points for redundancy. Most climbers are leery to trust *two* hardware store fixtures and would never trust just one (like a single lap link) as the quality of the metallurgy is poor. When you come across one of these rap anchors featuring a mishmash of rusting chains and queer doodads, an easy way to give yourself an extra margin of safety is simply to tie a loop of nylon webbing through both bolt hangers as a backup.

While the two lengths of rusty chain would offer redundancy, it is lost where it all comes down to that one, measly lap link of unknown origin and vintage. Why trust your life to an aging hardware store relic some skinflint bought for 79 cents? This chain rig was easily backed up by threading a length of 1-inch webbing through both bolt hangers and tying it with a water knot. Though serious, these hardware store horror shows are rarely fatal owing to the modest loads generated by rappelling. As belay anchors, such setups are truly widow makers.

Rap rings. Left to right: FIXE stainless steel (12,500 pounds), SMC aluminum (3,400 pounds), Ushba titanium (6,750 pounds).

The American "death" triangle is something of a myth when it comes to rappel anchors. The fear is that this setup multiplies the loading force by pulling the bolts together. Under body weight the angle of the sling, at both bolts, is about 90 degrees. This is poor engineering by any definition. But given that rap anchors basically sustain body-weight loads, the American triangle, though always a wretched rigging strategy, is by and large only deadly when rigged to abysmal primary anchors.

Now we're talking—much better than the American triangle. Here we have two slings, fed independently through each bolt, and two rap rings. With this narrow of an angle the load is distributed nearly 50/50 on the bolts.

Two 5-piece Rawl bolts installed with FIXE ring hangers. Such ring anchors are becoming more commonplace owing to brute strength, simple setup and fluid rope removal. Visually unobtrusive, the welded stainless rings are stronger than the hangers. Over time, however, the rings often show signs of wear—from people toproping and lowering directly off the rings, as well as from countless rappel ropes being pulled through the rings. Always inspect the rings for wear.

This two-bolt rap anchor is well engineered. All the components are stainless steel. Both bolts are 5-piece Rawls. The left one has a stainless steel FIXE hanger with stainless chain attached to a final quick link; the right bolt has a Petzl hanger with a quick link/welded stainless ring combo. The positioning of the bolts combined with the hardware rigging makes for a narrow angle of pull between the two bolts. Good to go.

This sturdy granite rock horn looks bomber: well attached, thick and solid rock. However, the tangle of old slings is stiff and degraded, the color faded from years in the sun. Worse is the fact that the sling is festooned with a single, hardware store quick link, providing no redundancy. If you find yourself on trad routes that may necessitate rappels from natural features such as trees and rock features, prepare yourself with a small knife, some spare nylon webbing and rap rings to re-rig old tat like this.

This setup is ideal save that the slings are too short and don't achieve enough coverage behind the top of the flake. If the rappeller should bounce or swing about during descent, the slings might shift on the anchor and slip off the left-hand, rounded edge of the flake.

That's what we're talking about. Two longer slings of 1-inch tubular nylon webbing tied with water knots, rigged with two rap rings. If you don't know the water knot, learn it (see the knots chapter). Many accidents have occurred with webbing rigged at anchors when some funky knot (something other than the water knot or double fisherman's) came untied. One knot that has failed in several instances (with fatal consequences) is the flat overhand, probably loosely tied and with no tail.

FOR THE LAST TIME . . .

Conforming an anchor to the letter of every sound principle does not guarantee that the anchor will hold a single pound. The best rigging can do no more than exploit the potential holding strength of the primary placements. Hence the first rule in building all anchors is to get sound primary placements. With bomber primary placements, the rules of thumb and modern rigging methods stack the odds in our favor that the anchor will do its job and do it well.

About the Authors

John Long is the author of twenty-five books, with over one million copies in print. He is the principal author of the How to Rock Climb series. His short-form literary stories have been widely anthologized and translated into many languages. John won the 2006 Literary Award for excellence in alpine literature from the American Alpine Club.

PHOTO COURTESY OF
JOHN LONG

PHOTO COURTESY OF BOB GAINES

Bob Gaines is an AMGA Certified Rock Guide who has been teaching rock climbing since 1983. He is the owner/director of Vertical Adventures Climbing School, based at Joshua Tree National Park, California, where he has taught clients ranging from Boy Scouts to Navy Seals. Bob has also worked extensively as a climbing stunt coordinator on over forty television commercials. He was the chief safety officer for the movie *Cliffhanger* and doubled for Captain Kirk when Kirk free soloed El Capitan in *Star Trek V*. Bob is also the co-author of *Rock Climbing Tahquitz and Suicide Rocks* (The Globe Pequot Press, 2001).